Hidden in His Own Story

Hidden in His Own Story

~

Discovering Jesus
in the Parables
of the Gospels

ANDREW WALTON

RESOURCE *Publications* · Eugene, Oregon

Resource Publications
An Imprint of Wipf and Stock Publishers
199 W. 8th Ave., Suite 3
Eugene, OR 97401

www.wipfandstock.com

PAPERBACK ISBN: 978-1-5326-0758-5
HARDCOVER ISBN: 978-1-5326-0760-8
EBOOK ISBN: 978-1-5326-0759-2

Manufactured in the U.S.A.   11/21/16

Contents

Acknowledgments

Writing seems like such a solitary effort until it is time to consider all of the people who in one way or another are involved in the process. It's much like the two professions in which I've spent most of my life: the theater and the church. Both are collaborative ventures requiring the passion and talents of many imaginative and creative people seeking Truth. I owe much, perhaps even my life, to both institutions.

In over twenty-five years of pastoral ministry, three wonderful congregations in Georgia, Washington DC, and Florida have afforded me patience, freedom, and love as I tried out bits and pieces of this manuscript in sermons and classes. My most sincere thanks go to the good people of Forsyth Presbyterian Church, Capitol Hill Presbyterian Church, and Trinity Clearwater Presbyterian Church.

I would never have survived in ministry if not for the support and friendship of other pastors too numerous to mention individually. However several groups do need acknowledgment: the ecumenical coffee klatch in Forsyth, the Macon lectionary group, the Monday Macon group, the Capitol Hill lectionary support group, S-3 Cohorts at Columbia Seminary, and the Estes Park Pastors Retreat gang. Personal mention goes to my good friend and colleague

Acknowledgments

Byron Buck, who is always there as a sounding board. I have unending gratitude for the friendship, support, and love of my colleagues, mentors, and brothers Philip "Skip" Dunford, Bill Owens, and Jeff Sockwell for over twenty-eight years.

There are several people who helped me with the manuscript by offering feedback and suggestions. Chief among them is my friend Sally Galbraith, who edited early drafts with keen eye and ear to help me find my writing voice, but more importantly the voice of Jesus in his stories. Also reading the manuscript and offering their encouragement were friends, colleagues, and mentors Walter Brueggemann and Joan Gray. Of course I must give thanks and gratitude for the fine people at Wipf and Stock Publishers for bringing the book to publication.

Mostly, I can't even imagine this project coming to life without the loving support of my number one proofreader, editor, and soul monitor, my love, my compass, and life companion, Peg Walton.

Finally, I thank you the reader, for without you there is only one side to this conversation we call writing. I appreciate that you are already reading this, which tells me you are a fellow seeker and explorer of the mysteries and truths of faith. Thank you for coming along on this pilgrimage of discovering God's Presence and Light in our lives.

Prelude

Dried blood encrusted my eyes. Each breath was more and more shallow. Every attempt to move my arms or legs produced pure anguish. How long had I been there? How long would it take for life to slowly drain from my body? Would I die beaten, bloodied, naked, and alone in the scorching sun?

I remembered walking along the path from Jerusalem to Jericho, the morning sun in my face as it rose over a distant hill, and the silhouetted faces of two approaching strangers. Then all went black.

Voices. Was I delirious? They grew louder and clearer. Thank God! I cried out, "Help!" Instead, an animal-like groan pierced the air as pain shot through my jaw. I tried again. The pain was white, the sound inhuman.

"Stay away," one of the voices said.

"But he needs help, master," responded another.

"Perhaps," said the first, "but not from us. He is unclean. Do as I say. Stay clear of him and move along."

"No!" I cried out, but only in my mind. As the two figures walked away, for a brief moment the sun caught the bottom of their robes. One was coarse and plain, that of a servant. The other was fine linen. Gold trim on the hem sparkled in the sunlight, the unmistakable garb of a temple priest.

"I am one of you," my mind shouted. "I am a son of Abraham. Where is your mercy?" The two figures disappeared into the shadows. I was lost.

I lay there for what could have been minutes or hours before I heard other voices approaching. If only I could speak.

"Is he alive?" one asked.

"I think not," came a reply. "The insects are already having their way. We best stay away."

"I agree. As Levites we must maintain our purity."

"Poor man."

"Yes."

They walked away and the sun returned. Their only mercy had been a brief moment of cool shade in their shadows.

My eyes closed for what I thought would be the last time. Ringing in my head subsided to the hum of insects crawling about my face, but I could do nothing. The sun beat down, yet I shivered as cold welled up within. Gasping for breath my body stilled, the pain gone. "So, this is death?" Darkness gently caressed me.

When the mind goes to sleep it is as the scriptures say, "A thousand years are like a watch in the night." It could have been a few moments or eternity itself. I don't really know. I do know that the cool darkness surrounding me became a cool sensation on my forehead and lips. Then in the distant dark there was a light.

The light moved toward me. Or was I moving toward the light? I had no way of knowing for all points of reference were gone. The light grew larger and brighter and at some point I saw a figure within the light, inviting me into the light. There were no words yet I could hear a voice within, "Don't be afraid. I am here with you. You are safe."

The voice filled me with peace and wholeness. Then I saw the figure's face, a face of pure kindness, compassion, and love. I entered the light and in doing so, became the light. I knew I was in the Presence of God and could stay there forever.

The light blinded, but the figure's shadow covered and protected me. The voice came from within, distant and faint growing ever louder.

"Don't be afraid. I am here with you. You are safe."

The coolness on my lips and forehead returned. Someone washed my face. Dried blood cleared from my eyes and they opened. The light was the blazing sun. The shadow of a man bent over me and said, "Be still. You are injured. I am here to help you."

I tried to talk but the intense pain in my jaw allowed only grotesque sounds. The man gently put one hand over my mouth and with the other raised one finger to his lips.

"No need to talk just now."

His face came into focus, the face I had seen in the light, filled with kindness and compassion. Again, I felt the wholeness, the Presence of God.

Like a physician examining a patient, he touched my body in several places and asked each time.

"Is this painful?"

All I could manage in response were whispered sounds resembling "yes" and "no." Each time I tried to say more he gently placed one hand on my mouth and raised a finger of the other to his lips.

We soon discovered that the most painful places were my ribs and jaw, both probably broken. The rest of my body was badly bruised, bloodied and sore, with several lacerations, especially around my face. Soon I was sitting up as he soothed my wounds with oil and wine.

"Can you ride?" he asked, pointing to a donkey standing a few feet away.

I nodded, not really knowing whether I could or not.

He helped me to my feet and on to the donkey. Pain filled my body. My head began to spin. Lying across the donkey's back, blood rushed to my head. Again there was merciful darkness.

The next thing I remember were the voices of the Stranger and another man. They both took me from the donkey and into a house. Inside they lay me on a soft pallet where the Stranger again gently poured water in my clenched mouth and nursed my wounds with oil and wine.

"You are safe now," he said to me.

I looked into his face filled with light, and I knew I was safe.

In semiconsciousness I heard the Stranger and the other man talking. It soon became clear we were at an inn and the man was the innkeeper.

The Stranger gave him some money and said, "Please care for him and when I return I will repay you whatever you spend."

"What is his name?" the innkeeper asked.

That's when I realized that the Stranger had never once asked for my name or where I was from.

"I don't know," the Stranger said. "Perhaps you can discover this when he is able to talk."

The Stranger came to me, looked into my eyes and said softly, "Don't be afraid. You are safe." The same words the figure in the light had used. His face then became that now familiar light of love. And then he added, "You were lost but now found, dead but now alive."

Prelude

I wanted the Stranger to know who I was. I tried to say my name, but the words stayed in my mind.

As the Stranger turned to leave, I spoke but no one heard me. "I am Jesus. Jesus of Nazareth."

Then he was gone, but I was not afraid and I knew I was safe for I had been in the Presence of God . . .

Selah

The Backstory

The most enigmatic person in the history of Western civilization was Jesus of Nazareth. The fact that he lived cannot be escaped. Western culture has even arranged time itself according to before or after the time when Jesus lived. The influence of his life has been unavoidable for over two thousand years, yet, little to nothing is known about his actual life. Exactly who was this man?

This observation is nothing new. Quite the contrary, the quest and search for the historical Jesus has been going on for several centuries and in earnest since the eighteenth century. The myriad of writings on the subject is overwhelming. One can discover with a trip to any theological library, or better yet with several clicks of a mouse, a plethora of theories, analyses, and conjectures about the historical Jesus.

Yet among all the scholarship and words, all we really know about the man, Jesus of Nazareth, beyond what is in the Bible and other religious texts, is that he lived, had a brother named James, and was crucified by the Roman prefect Pontius Pilate for insurrection. We know these things primarily from two brief extrabiblical references, one the Jewish historian Flavius Josephus,[1] and the other

1. *Wikipedia.com*, s.v. "Josephus on Jesus."

the Roman historian Tacitus.[2] All else we know about Jesus comes from people who believed him to be the Messiah to the Jewish people and/or the Christ of Christianity—God in the flesh. In most cases these "believers" are quite up front about making a case for their beliefs.

Conversational Stories

The following pages are not a search for the historical Jesus or a critique of traditional Christian belief, but rather a different perspective on how we may experience both through conversational stories. Conversational stories are the stories we tell as we share experience of our lives within the give and take of conversation. These stories often lie just beneath the surface of crafted stories told about someone rather than by them. As we imaginatively unveil events and personal experiences behind and within the artistically construed stories told by and about Jesus in the Bible, a different perspective on Jesus emerges.

In the South, where I am from, storytelling is as natural as breathing. Having been born into, nurtured by, and participated in a storytelling family and culture, I find my conversations usually center on, or eventually come around to, stories. The majority of these are not made-up tales but recollections of actual life experiences.

Conversational stories are personal. Most stories are about the one telling the story, either directly or indirectly. We have a tendency to tell our own stories.

It is conversational because one story usually leads to another. This may even be the essence of what makes a "good" story, that it elicits a story within the life of the listener.

2. *Wikipedia.com*, s.v. "Tacitus on Christ."

Now, imagine personal, conversational stories in the life of Jesus, as he walks along a path with his disciples, or shares a meal with them, or as they sit under a night sky wondering, remembering, and telling their own stories. Imagine these stories then becoming what we now know as the parables and teachings of and about Jesus.

By imagining some of Jesus' parables and teachings as his own stories we open a window that allows a glimpse into what may have been actual experiences in Jesus' life, telling us more about who he was as a person, giving us more insight into how he became the mysterious, mythical person who changed the world.

As the enigma of a mythical Messiah and Christ fades, we realize we know more than we know we know, and discover a more human Jesus hidden within his own story.

When I was studying biblical Greek in seminary our professor, Wayne Merritt, ended most classes with a phrase of encouragement as he smiled wryly and looked out at confused faces and glazed eyes. "You know more than you know you know."

I offer these same words of encouragement to you as we look at a few familiar parables, teachings, and stories by and about Jesus. By making a slight shift in perspective and viewing these experiences and events as if they were actually life events of Jesus, a portrait of the man Jesus begins to appear. Then our own stories begin to emerge from Jesus' story and we really do know more that we know we know.

Primal Story

Regardless of all the things we do not know about the historical Jesus, one thing is certain. Jesus was a storyteller. He told stories in response to questions, stories when teaching, stories about the past, stories about the future, and even stories about other stories. In the gospels his stories were rarely if ever abstract, but rather grounded in human experiences and told with the purpose of communicating some aspect of compassion, love, power, abandonment, greed, generosity, suffering, death, grace, patience, and forgiveness.

There is also a dynamic at work in the gospels in which Jesus and his stories are the main subject of a story told by someone else who has their own purposes and perspectives. The gospels, both canonical and noncanonical, all have their own passions and prejudices encumbered with vested interest in presenting Jesus and his stories in a way as to promote particular presuppositions.

What is now known in biblical scholarship as narrative criticism evolved out of this dynamic of identifying and exploring the elements and craft of storytelling in the Bible and other texts. However, before and behind the formal study of biblical stories are the stories themselves both individually as narrative units and collectively as meta-narrative which can also be understood as "primal story," the story from which other stories grow.

In his book *The Bible Makes Sense*, Walter Brueggemann expands on previous assertions of German Old Testament scholar Gerhard von Rad and English New Testament scholar C. H. Dodd, that the Bible has its roots in two primal narratives—the exodus and the resurrection. Brueggemann says a primal narrative is "the most important story we know, and we have come to believe it is decisively about us."[3] He goes on to say that "von Rad has made it clear that these assertions come behind and before any reasoned theology or any apologetic concern to justify faith

3. Brueggemann, *The Bible Makes Sense*, rev. ed. (Louisville: Westminster John Knox, 2001), 23–26.

to outsiders."[4] In other words, the primal story is contained in every other story, past and present, and is the portal through which every other story is filtered.

Primal stories (yes, we can and do have more than one) are so powerful that they shape everything happening afterward. Primal stories also change the past by becoming a lens through which we see and reimagine everything prior to their telling. The future emanates from the primal story and the past leads up to it.

We All Have Primal Stories

The Bible is not the only place we find primal stories. We all have primal stories in our lives and communities that literally define who we are: death, birth, marriage, divorce, a love affair, achievement, failure, sickness, injury, epiphany, and abandonment. The list is endless, as are life's experiences.

In order for people to really know who we are it is important for us to tell and hear our respective primal stories. The same is true for our knowing Jesus. The way we come to really know the person Jesus is through his stories and particularly his primal stories.

A Man Hidden in His Own Story

Of course Jesus never actually says, "This is the central story of my life from which the past and future emanate." However, if we accept the premise that the parables and teachings of Jesus are his personal tales, we now have a collection of stories in which we can identify topics, themes, and characters. Also, the detail and care with which a story is told is usually an indicator of that story's importance to

4. Ibid, 24.

the teller. By observing and exploring all of Jesus' stories and teachings we begin to see common elements and can then imagine one or more of these stories as the source from which all the others come.

Emerging from the whole of Jesus' stories and teachings are several common elements, including but not limited to healing, forgiveness, persistence, faith, kindness, fairness, generosity, and love; all grounded in compassion, but not compassion as mere empathy. Rather, the compassion described of Jesus in the gospels, *splagchnizomai*, which literally means "to be moved in the bowels," the bowels believed to be the seat of love and pity. One can imagine *splagchnizomai* as intense, visceral emotion akin to suffering that is prompted by another's suffering. In numerous stories of healing Jesus is reported to have *splagchnizomai* toward the individuals as well as crowds of people who are made whole.

Such compassion opens up vistas of hospitality, liberation, regeneration, and new life. Jesus, being fully human, can be assumed as not unlike most people in that he would have told stories which came from his own experiences, passions, prejudices, and perspectives of compassion.

A Note to the Reader

The reimagined story that follows is drawn from parables and teachings attributed to Jesus, as well as events recorded in the four gospels. The actual Scripture passages from which the story emerges appear in the appendix in approximate order of reference.

There are no chapter titles or numbers but rather pauses between stories within The Story, indicated with the Hebrew word *Selah* that is used throughout the Psalms and is believed to mean "pause and consider."

I've written this story as an invitation for you to re-consider and reimagine both the humanity and divinity of Jesus. My invitation goes out to people who are not familiar with the Bible stories and have only heard them through other sources. It also goes out to many who have rejected traditional interpretations of the stories as religious dogma. I also extend the invitation to many people who are so steeped in the stories that they have become cliché.

Even the most clever storyteller or writer of fiction can never totally disguise or deny their personal influence on the story. And most of us have had the experience of someone beginning a story with, "I know a person who . . ." when in fact that "person" is the one telling the story. Why not imagine the same when Jesus says, "Once there was a man traveling on the way from Jerusalem to Jericho? . . ."

Selah

The Story

When the sun goes down in the desert and darkness caresses the earth, the warmth of day quickly becomes the cold of night. As the brilliant colors of the sunset fade to black, the heavens awaken. A clear desert sky overwhelms one with mystery and awe.

We sat under such a sky with a roaring fire between us. Weary and needing sleep, I wanted to lay my head on the ground and dream, but the voice on the other side of the flame was insistent.

"Tell me your story, Jesus." The voice appeared to come from the flames that pierced the darkness and dispelled the cold.

"My story? What do you mean by 'my story'?"

"Tell me who you are, Jesus of Nazareth, son of Joseph and Mary."

"You know who I am."

"Perhaps. But do you?"

My response surprised me, "I'm not so sure anymore—who I am."

"So tell me your story, from as far back as you can remember."

Selah

Mystery was no stranger to my mother. She saw the world through eyes of wonder and by doing so made life wonderful. To her nothing was ever simply as it appeared. There was always something else behind, in, and through what most people saw as plain, ordinary, or even dull. Sunlight sang, plants and flowers danced, water played, and the moon and stars held secrets of time. There were times when she looked at me with the same wonder. She had reason to know the world this way.

Mother worked hard at taking care of our family. She cooked, sewed, cleaned, shopped at the market, and brought water from the well. Not only did she work hard she did everything with a joyful spirit, even the most difficult tasks, as if she carried a secret deep within that permeated her life with joy.

When preparing the food for our family, she was particularly joyous. One day as she prepared flour for baking bread she took a small jar from a hole in the earthen floor. From the jar she pinched a small bit of powder, sprinkled it in the flour, and then began mixing.

"Mother, what are you putting in the flour?"

"It is yeast, son. It leavens the dough."

"Leavens?"

"Yes. You know how sometimes our bread is flat like the bread we eat at Passover. That bread is just flour, water and a little salt. Then there are other times when we have the bread you like so much."

"Yes, the light fluffy bread in a large loaf."

"This is what yeast does. Just a tiny bit mixed in the dough makes it grow into a nice, light, round shape."

"How does it do this?"

"I really don't know. I just know it does."

"Like magic!"

"Maybe," she laughed.

"But why do you hide it?"

She smiled broadly and chuckled at my childlike questioning, "I'm not really hiding it. It needs to be kept in a cool dark place in order to stay fresh and keep its 'magic' as you call it."

"Is yeast like salt?"

"Not really. Salt is used to make food taste better and to preserve it. But yeast and salt are very much alike in two ways. It only takes a tiny bit of either, and both can lose their 'magic' if not cared for properly."

She smiled and put her arms around me. The secret joy of her life spilled into the room surrounding and holding us both the way she was holding me. Her smile, her joy, her touch was the yeast and salt of my life. And just like yeast and salt, the magic of her love filled and encompassed my soul.

Selah

Rarely did I ever know my mother to be overly anxious or afraid. However, on those occasions when she was anxious the joy that she normally exuded was transformed into intense determination and persistence.

One night I awoke to my parents' voices.

"Mary, what are you doing?" Papa whispered so as not to wake my brother, sister, and me.

"I've lost something." Her voice was hushed and deliberate. I saw her sweeping the floor by lamplight.

"But what could be so important. Wouldn't it be easier to find in the daylight?" Papa asked.

"It probably would. But I dropped a coin to the floor just before lying down to sleep and after putting out the lamp. It is the only money we have and will buy our food for several days. I cannot rest or sleep until I find it."

"Can I help?" Papa sighed.

"You go back to sleep. There is no need for you to worry. I will find it."

From the shadows, on the edge of the lamplight I saw her search for that lost coin. As anxious as she was, she remained calm and focused. My own anxiety began to subside.

I had seen that confident belief before and could hear her saying to me, "Jesus, if you believe something with all your soul and mind and body you will see your belief become reality."

"How do I do this, Mother?" I had asked.

"First you feel it deeply, next you think it thoroughly, and then you take action as if it is already done."

I fell asleep knowing she would find the coin because she believed she would.

I awoke to laughter in the courtyard outside our house. Mother told her friends about sweeping for hours in the lamplight and finally finding the lost coin. Her voice filled the air with joy.

I breathed in the joy of her laughter and also the strength of her faith, and secretly thought, "That coin was never lost because my mother always believed it would be found."

Selah

There was a passing phrase my parents would say to one another when they thought no one was listening. "Remember the angels," one would say to the other, especially when an important decision loomed before them. The first time I remember hearing it I was twelve years old and we had gone on our annual Passover trip to Jerusalem.

When the festival was ended they started home, but I was left behind in Jerusalem. Assuming that I was in the group of travelers, they had gone a day's journey before noticing I was missing. They looked among our relatives and friends, but didn't find me, so they left my brother and sister with family and returned to Jerusalem.

When I realized they were gone I asked around about my parents and our pilgrimage group. I was scared and frantic. One of the temple teachers named Gamaliel saw I was about to strike out after them. He calmed me down by saying my parents would most assuredly return for me, and until they did I could stay in the temple.

It ended up taking them three days to find me. By then I had gotten to know many of the teachers. They let me sit and listen as they discussed and argued the Torah and the Prophets. After a day or so, and not knowing any better, I began to ask some questions. At first some of the teachers were rather annoyed, but Gamaliel encouraged them to let me participate.

I thought my questions were rather obvious, but a few of the teachers were astonished at my knowledge of the scriptures as well as my willingness to question some traditional interpretations, especially those having to do with the treatment of poor people and people outside our tradition. Being on the inside of the temple for only a few days was enough to see how wealthy, powerful people received better treatment than the poor, sick and outcaste.

When my parents finally returned, my mother, obviously upset, ran toward me and swept me into her arms, nearly crushing me as her tears wet my neck.

"Jesus, where have you been? Your Papa and I have been frantically searching for you. We were afraid something bad had happened to you."

Papa walked straight past me and began apologizing to the group of teachers, who immediately pulled him aside where a hushed conversation ensued. As they finished talking, Papa turned and walked toward me, his eyes piercing through me.

"Son, do you see how upset your mother is?"

"Yes, Papa. I'm sorry. I didn't know when you left. I was frightened and the teachers said I could stay here. They said you would know to find me here."

Mother quickly stood between Papa and me with her back to me as Papa continued to stare at me over her shoulder. That's when I heard her pleading whisper, "Remember the angels, Joseph."

For the first time, I knew my parents had a secret they were not telling me. I also knew then was not the time to ask about it.

Selah

Papa was a natural builder. Give him some wood and stone and he could build anything from a great temple to a modest house or a simple table or stool. He never had formal training and always said he learned most of what he knew from his father. This is probably the reason he was always teaching my brother and me as we worked alongside.

When he told us to do something, not only did he show us how, but in time would explain why things were done in a certain way. We learned about things being level and plumb, the importance of angles, the strength of triangles and arches, the placement and pressure in laying stones or bricks, and the proper use and care of tools. Working with Papa was a lot like going to school.

His first and foremost lesson was, "Always build on a good foundation," which usually meant hard work for my brother and me, digging until we reached solid rock. Once my brother asked, "Why can't we just put some rocks on top of the ground and use them for the foundation?"

Papa laughed, "You do that, then come back after the first rainy season and see if your house is still straight and strong, or even standing at all. If you want it to last through the storms, keep digging! Have I ever told you the story of the tower of Siloam that fell and killed eighteen people?"

"Only a hundred times!" I said.

"No! Not again!" My brother feigned exasperation.

We all laughed knowing he would probably tell it anyway, and it wouldn't be the last time. We wiped our brows, picked up our tools and kept digging.

Selah

～

Sometimes Papa went beyond Nazareth and Sepphoris to find work. Since this usually meant several days' journey, he would be away from home for extended periods of time. When I was old enough I would sometimes go with him, especially when he went to Tiberius by the sea.

At first sight from the top of Mt. Arbel I was enchanted. I was accustomed to water in buckets and jars drawn from springs and wells, not the enormous blue emerald that stretched in the distance below. Never had I imagined, much less seen, so much water. I had not yet seen the Great Sea, and when I eventually did it was in my eye and mind only a larger version of my first love, the Sea of Galilee.

In, around, and on the Sea of Galilee I discovered fishing. The first time I was there Papa and I were up before dawn so we could begin work at first light. On our way we passed a group of fishermen preparing their boats for a day of fishing. We watched for a while then as usual, Papa started a conversation.

"Pardon the interruption, but what are you doing to those nets?"

"We're mending them," one of the men replied.

"How do they get torn?"

"On rocks and limbs." The man seemed to be slightly annoyed.

By this time we had walked toward the boat and were standing next to it. "Sorry to bother you," Papa said. "We don't know much about fishing. I'm a carpenter and stone mason from Nazareth."

"What brings you to Galilee?" another man asked.

"I have to go where the work is," Papa said.

"I guess we're lucky that our work stays right here in this water," the first man replied as he offered his hand to Papa. "My name is Zebedee."

"It's good to meet you, Zebedee. I'm Joseph and this is my son Jesus. He works with me sometimes to help and to learn the trade."

"I have two sons about your age who also help and hopefully learn about fishing." Zebedee said, looking at me. "They should be here soon."

And sure enough, they soon appeared. James was a little older than me, and John slightly younger. They jumped onto the boat and waved for me to join them. I looked to Papa and he nodded permission. I scampered onto the boat. That's how quickly lifelong friendships begin.

James and John quickly began their jobs of putting nets and ropes in place, all the time answering my questions about why they were doing this or that. Papa and Zebedee stood on the shore talking about building things and fishing, and Roman soldiers and taxes.

Eventually Papa said, "It's time to go, Jesus. I hate to break up your fun but we have work to do."

This prompted a unison sigh from all three of us, with James and John pleading, "Does he have to go?"

Papa and Zebedee looked at each other as if to say, "It's OK with me if it's OK with you."

"Why don't you let him go out with us? We'll be back in by midafternoon."

This time Papa looked at me. My pleading eyes must have been convincing. "Very well. I can get through one day without your help. Here, you'll need this." He tossed me a small bundle containing my lunch.

The boat glided across the still, glistening water as the sun appeared over distant hills on the far shore. The only sounds were Zebedee's oars dipping in and out of the water and birds overhead that followed in hope of a hearty meal.

When we reached the spot where we were to fish, James and John, without any instruction from their father, immediately began to get the net ready to cast. Zebedee watched the surface of the water as if he could see what was underneath. Soon he pointed to a spot that looked like any other and said, "There." Then with gentle and silent movement of the oars he slowly guided the boat to the spot and nodded to his sons. James and John threw the net just beyond the spot and it disappeared into the water. In just a few seconds Zebedee said, "Pull it in."

They drew the net to the surface, which now churned violently as hundreds of flopping fish appeared. Something deep within me shifted. I would never again see the surface of water without thinking about the teeming life beneath that surface. I knew for the first time something I had sensed many times—beyond appearances lie unseen realities.

The net was so full James and John struggled to pull it in. John turned to me and yelled, "Don't just sit there! Give us a hand!" I grabbed a rope and pulled. Immediately I felt the weight of the fish.

"Keep pulling boys! It's a full one." Zebedee shouted.

The fish spilled into the boat, jumping and flopping everywhere. When the entire net was in we stood in fish up to our calves.

"Quickly now, small ones back into the water!" Zebedee instructed.

"How small?" I asked.

"The size of your hand." James said. "They won't sell so we must get them back into the water before they die."

"Then they grow and we catch them another day," laughed John.

"Too much talking, boys! Those fish won't jump back into the water themselves," shouted Zebedee. Even still, a few actually did flop back in the water.

After a few minutes of frantically throwing the smaller fish back into the water Zebedee said, "That's enough, boys. We'll sort out the rest when we get to shore."

"But won't they die?" I asked.

"Some at the bottom of the pile where there is a little water will live, but most will die." James answered.

"Why do you think those birds have been following us all day?" added John.

"That's a pretty good haul." Zebedee said as he surveyed the boat filled with fish. "We only have room for one more catch. You must be good luck, Jesus!" Everyone laughed. "James, John, get the net ready for one more cast. This time show Jesus how it's done and he can help cast it."

While Zebedee took the oars in search of another spot, James and John taught me how to gather the net and prepare it for another cast. All the while the movement within the pile of fish became still. It wasn't long before Zebedee said again, "There."

He was right about there being room for only one more net, but I'm not so sure about the luck part. We cast the net and again pulled it in. The lifeless pile of fish was again flopping and jumping with the new fish, now above our knees.

"That's all we can hold," Zebedee announced. "Let's separate them and get back to shore."

Once on the shore we separated the entire catch by size into large baskets to be taken to the market. There was also a basket for Zebedee's family where we threw some of the best fish. John was right about the birds that hovered overhead waiting for the occasional toss of a small fish or the chance to make a quick raid on one of the baskets.

When all the fish were in baskets and birds' bellies, and just as John, James, and I were finishing bailing fishy water from the hull, Papa walked up.

I heard his voice before seeing him. "How was the fishing today?" he asked in general. But I answered.

"It was great, Papa, great! Look at all the fish we caught."

"I think your carpenter is also a fisherman, Joseph," Zebedee shouted to Papa as they both laughed.

"Will I ever get him back on the land?" Papa mused as he smiled at me. And somewhere deep inside I knew he was right.

That was my first time on a boat and that day the sea became a part of me, opening windows into awareness that somehow I was connected to both land and sea in ways I had never imagined.

The shining surface of the sea deceives by concealing a vast unseen world. Its peaceful beauty is equaled, if not surpassed, by its vibrant, life-giving utility. Beneath the glittering waves that reflect both sun and moon is a world inhabited by countless varieties of fish and plants surrounded by life-giving water in the same way that the air we breathe surrounds people, animals, and plants.

In time, I also discovered the sea's ruthless volatility. During a storm, within minutes, the smooth, glassy surface can become churning waves large enough to swamp large fishing boats, capsize smaller ones, and swallow fishermen. The sea teaches one gratitude as well as respect. It gives life and takes life.

Selah

One hot summer day when my brother and I were boys, we had been playing among the hills between Sepphoris and Nazareth. On the way home we stopped to visit a good friend, a mustard bush that had grown into a large tree. We loved to sit in its shade and rest.

Its leaves shimmered in the warm breeze animating the old tree as if it were dancing. Small birds flittered about within its branches, taking shelter from the sun, just like us. Maybe some of them lived in the tree. A trail of ants made their way on its trunk, disappearing up into its limbs, and down into its roots.

"I wonder how old this tree is," my brother mused.

"It's very old," I said. "Mustard bushes don't grow this big overnight. I wonder if it knows how old it is."

The wise old tree had seen many sunrises and sunsets and provided shelter for countless people, animals, insects, and birds. Through scorching sun, driving rain, relentless wind, as well as gentle breezes and morning dews, it stood as its own proclamation of heaven on earth.

"It reminds me of a psalm," I said, "the one that says, '. . . planted by streams of water, which yield their fruit in its season, and their leaves do not wither. In all that they do, they prosper.'"

I imagined a time long ago when the mustard tree had not been there. The place it occupied, the sky above and earth below, had been empty. Then I saw one of the tree's seeds on the ground, picked it up, and placed it in the palm of my hand. It was so tiny. Showing it to my brother, I said, "Just think, at one time this great tree was a tiny seed like this one."

"I wonder how it got here and who planted it."

"Maybe it clung to the sandal of a passing traveler," I said.

"Or fell from someone's bag of spices," my brother added.

"Or the wind carried it for miles before dropping it here."

"However it got here," my brother said, "it found welcoming soil and just like the psalm says, it prospered."

We laughed, then wondered and imagined that the tree under which we rested was once the possibility and potential within a tiny seed.

"Look," my brother said, pointing to my hand. "You're holding a great tree in your hand."

Laughing, I said, "Let's plant it."

"But where? There's already a tree here."

"I don't know yet. On the way home we'll find a place with good soil that looks like it needs a tree. Some day many years from now two other boys will sit under it and wonder where it came from and who planted its seed."

Selah

Our family subsided on what money Papa could make by his skills as a carpenter and stonemason. He and my brother and I, when we were old enough, usually had plenty of work in Sepphoris where Herod was building a city to honor himself. The work was steady but the pay meager. Papa handed over what little he earned to Mother who was a wise and shrewd household manager. She even managed to regularly put a little aside.

The walk from Nazareth to Sepphoris was only a few miles so we would come and go regularly. We were well acquainted with the journey. So much so that sometimes for an adventure we would leave the worn path to walk across the hillsides, which also became familiar. A wealthy man in Sepphoris who really didn't care if people trespassed owned much of that land. It was mostly rocky and dry, making it habitable primarily to small plants and animals, providing the land its own beauty and purpose.

My brother and I loved playing among the rocks. Papa would often tell us stories about playing among the hills when he as a boy growing up in Nazareth. But there was one story he kept to himself.

One day the talk around Sepphoris was that the wealthy landowner had died and his son had inherited all of his property.

The son, as sons often do, announced that he was selling much of his inherited property, including those rocky hillsides between Nazareth and Sepphoris. There were jokes and laughter about the son's audacity in thinking anyone would want to own such unproductive land. But Papa didn't join in the laughter. He only listened and smiled.

One night soon after the landowner's death and the son's announcement, we heard the voices of our parents, animated and tense, speaking in hushed tones so as not to disturb our sleep.

"Have you gone mad, Joseph?"

"I know it sounds crazy but I must do this. I have thought of it nearly every day since that day as a boy."

"But how do you know it's still there?"

"I know. I've been by the spot thousands of times and it remains undisturbed."

"And what if it's not. We could lose everything we own for nothing but a pile of rocks."

"Mary, remember the angels. You must trust me, Mary. I know this in my heart."

There was a long silence then Mother replied. "Joseph, I have not heard nor seen this kind of urgent passion in you since your dream took us off to Egypt when Jesus was a child. I can see there is no persuading you otherwise. Very well. Go to sleep now. The morning will show us the way."

I fell back asleep wondering just what the coming dawn had in store for our family.

The following morning both Papa and Mother said there was something my brother and I should know. "The next few days will seem rather strange and perhaps frightening. We are selling our home and possessions and going to live with Mother's cousin Elizabeth for a while. During this time we can only ask you to trust and not questions us. You must know one thing. Regardless of where we live, your Mother and I will be with you and you will be safe."

And so it was. Papa even sold his tools, except for a pickax and a spade. Within a few days, everything we had but a few clothes and personal items was gone, and we were living with cousin Elizabeth.

Then one day Papa and Mother both went to Sepphoris while we stayed at Elizabeth's house. They returned as anxious as sheep that know a fox or wolf is lurking about. The very next morning all of us headed out for Sepphoris, with me carrying Papa's pickax and my brother holding the spade, and my baby sister in Mother's arms.

In Sepphoris we didn't go to our normal places, but rather to the large house of the wealthy landowner, which now belonged to his son. Servants ushered Papa, Mother, and little sister in while we waited outside.

Some men with whom my Papa worked recognized us. One of them called out, "Has your old father gone mad, boys?"

"Watch what you say, my brother shouted back?"

"Are you going to use that axe and spade to clear off that worthless pile of rocks he is buying?"

"What are you talking about?" I asked.

"Don't you know? He's buying some of that God-forsaken land between here and Nazareth," one of the men replied.

Another quickly added, "And if that's not crazy enough, he's buying the steepest, most barren and rocky parcel."

Still another chimed in, "You'll need more than a pickax and shovel."

The Story

All of the men laughed as they walked away. My face burned with anger at the men, confusion at what they had said, and shame at being laughed at. My brother's face contorted with bewilderment. We were stunned and silent, not knowing what to say to one another.

Papa and Mother came from the house. I immediately asked, "Papa, please tell us what is going on. Some men just came by and said you are buying some worthless land. Is this why we sold our home and possessions?"

"They are correct, son. And here is the deed." He held up a piece of freshly inked parchment. "Now, grab that pickax and spade and let's go find out what we just bought."

The men were right. It was the steepest, rockiest, most barren part of the land. But it was a place my brother and I had been many times as we climbed and played among the rocks on the way to and from work with Papa. But why in the world would Papa buy such a place? And how could Mother allow him to do it?

When we arrived at a familiar clearing at the top of the highest hill, Papa said, "Jesus, James sit down on those big rocks there with your Mother and sister and listen."

"When I was a boy, even younger that you are now, I often came out to these hills to play and be alone. I know both of you do this sometimes as well. One day as I played among these very rocks I heard voices coming up the hill. I hid behind that big rock right over there and watched as several men entered the clearing.

A man wearing fine robes and sashes led them. Later I learned the man was the owner of this land, the man who died recently. The men following him carried three large urns and digging tools.

They stopped here in this clearing and the landowner instructed the men to bury the urns. It took several hours because of the rocky soil. When the hole was big enough they put the urns inside and buried them, finally placing three large stones over the spot.

The landowner said to the men words I have never forgotten, "No one, not even my wife, my son, nor sons and daughters yet born, is to ever know what we have done today. I hold each of you responsible with your life for keeping this secret."

"Are the urns still buried here, Papa?" I asked.

"I have watched this spot for many years and not one stone has ever been moved."

"What's inside them?" my brother asked.

"I'm not sure," replied Papa. "But soon after I saw them buried the talk around Sepphoris was that the landowner had recently lost much of his fortune in an inopportune business venture, and that he had tuned over management of his remaining wealth to his son. Within a few years the son rebuilt that fortune and more. But there was never another word about how the first fortune was lost.

I believe that long forgotten "inopportune business venture" is buried beneath the very stones on which you sit, and which your mother and I now own." He held up the parchment deed. "So, let's get busy digging and discover if any of this is true."

It was true. As we pried open the first urn gold coins glimmered in the sunlight. The second overflowed with precious stones of every imaginable color. The third revealed assorted plates, goblets, and candlesticks of gold, silver and brass. We all stood in silent amazement.

Papa turned to us, "My family, answers to our questions and the resources to fulfill our dreams are often closer than we ever imagine. Oftentimes to realize our dreams we must be patient and, when the time is right, willing to give up everything we own."

Selah

~

When Papa bought that "worthless" property and my brother and I saw those urns filled with riches we thought our days of hard work were over. Were we ever wrong!

The first thing to do was find a new home. Papa and Mother immediately acquired a plot of land and we built a small house, but larger than the one we had sold. Even though they could have easily hired someone else to build it, they insisted on us doing it ourselves.

Then came the animals. Mother had always wanted a herd of sheep and now she could have them. So, my brother and I became shepherd boys. We built a sheepfold on the outer edge of our land and purchased a few sheep for a beginning. It was now our job to care for the sheep, including taking them out regularly into the neighboring countryside to graze. Little did we know how much those sheep would teach us.

We thought we knew our way around the surrounding countryside. However, those sheep showed us crevices and cliffs we never knew existed or would have gone to even if we had known about them.

One day when we brought the sheep back into the sheepfold for the night, as usual, I herded and my brother counted. As the last one went through the gate, my brother announced, "There's one missing."

"There can't be," I replied. "We counted all one hundred before coming down the hill. Let's count again." But every time it came up the same, ninety-nine. After too many times through we were pretty sure which one was missing.

"I don't see Ishmael, anywhere," my brother said. To pass the time we would give the sheep names from the stories we had learned in the synagogue. Ishmael was an adventurous lamb that had only recently become old enough to go out with the entire herd. He had wandered off before. And, we had always discovered him missing before heading home.

"I'll go back up and find him," I sighed.

"We'll find him tomorrow," my brother said. "Mother has supper ready. Let's go in and eat."

"You know he won't make it through the night. I'll be lucky to find him alive anyway. But I must at least try."

"Do what you want. I'm going in for supper."

"Tell Mother and Papa I'll be back later." I threw my coiled rope over my shoulder, picked up my staff and satchel and headed back into the hills.

With only about an hour of daylight left, I didn't have much time. As soon as darkness sets in the predators begin to roam. I followed the path back to the place where we had last counted all one hundred, occasionally stopping to whistle and call out, "Ishmael! Ishmael!" Pausing to listen, I heard nothing but my own echo and the calls of distant birds.

By the time I got to the clearing where we had counted it was nearly dark and there had been no sign at all of the missing sheep. I looked around in the faint light for signs or tracks going off in another direction. That's when I saw something about fifty feet further up the hill in a direction where we had not gone that day. It was a small piece of wool on a bush. I walked a few feet farther, whistled and called out, "Ishmael!" Nothing. The wolves had probably already found him.

Just as I turned to go, a faint sound came from further up the hill. It was the unmistakable cry of a distressed sheep on the other side of a high cascade of large boulders.

Scrambling in the dark I slowly made my way up the rocks, whistling and calling. The sheep's cry became louder. Finally at the top, Ishmael's cry was loud and clear. Then, hearing and recognizing my voice, his cries became more constant and desperate. He must have fallen and was surely injured.

There was one problem. Ishmael's cries came from far below a steep cliff, and there was only one way to get to him, and that was straight down. In the dark it was difficult to tell how far down. My rope was only twenty feet long.

Looking and feeling around for an anchor, I found a bush with a thick trunk deeply embedded in a crevice of the rocks. With the rope securely tied to the bush, I tied my staff to the end of the rope and lowered it into the darkness. When it reached its end I started my descent into the unknown.

Protruding bushes that provided foot and handholds also scratched and scraped my arms and legs. Occasionally my outer cloak or satchel caught on a bush or protruding rock. I had thought of taking them off at the top, and now wished I had. All the while I talked to Ishmael so he could hear my voice. I also wondered and asked aloud, "How in the world did you get down there?"

I finally reached the staff at the end of my rope. Now, not only could I hear Ishmael's bleating but also his hoofs clicking against stone. He was only a few feet away but I had no more rope and no way of knowing if he was at the bottom or caught on a ledge. That's when I was glad I had brought my cloak and satchel.

With a good foothold and a protruding bush to hold onto with one hand I slipped my satchel off with the other. The satchel strap was long enough to go around my waist and tie off to the bush. This freed both hands allowing me to then untie my cloak and tie it to the end of the staff, giving me at least six to eight more feet which was just enough to reach Ishmael.

His desperate cries changed to joyous bleating. I dropped down beside him and put my arms round him. He was much smaller than I had remembered. I laughed until I cried, then we both whimpered into exhausted sleep.

First daylight revealed our perch, a large protruding ledge with another fifty feet of cliff below us. How that lamb got there I'll never know. He appeared uninjured. However, my arms, legs, and face were covered with scratches, cuts, and streaks of dried blood.

The ragtag lifeline of rope, staff, and cloak pointed the way back up. Not nearly as daunting in daylight, there were enough hand- and footholds that the rope would not have been necessary were it not for a lamb on my shoulders. Once at the top I put Ishmael on the ground and he scampered about as if all were normal.

Looking around and down, I realized I had been at the edge of that cliff before but never down into its bowels. From the top it provided one of the best views of the entire countryside. On that morning, as the rising sun's light spilled across the land, painting a magnificent vista, the view was particularly awesome. Breathing deeply I took it all in, looked up, and shouted, "Thank you!" Then we headed down the hill.

Soon Ishmael knew where he was and ran ahead and out of sight. Long before I could see them, I heard him and

the other sheep singing. He was back home, where I would
be soon. My heart swelled and overflowed with joy.

Selah

ᔐ

Even though I was the oldest son I always thought that my brother was Papa's favorite. Of course Papa never came out and said it, but it was apparent in the way he looked at him, the way he always overlooked his shortcomings, and rarely held him to the same standards expected of me. There was tenderness between them that I envied and craved, a bond between father and son I had never felt.

What I thought at the time was the ultimate insult came when Papa sat us both down and explained that he did not intend to follow our Hebrew tradition of the full inheritance going to the elder son.

His words, like stones, pounded me to the ground, "Each of you, my sons, will receive equal shares of the modest wealth I have accumulated." Equal! I knew what equal felt like. My brother was Cain, Jacob, Isaac, Joseph, Moses, David, and Solomon. I was Abel, and Esau, and Ishmael, and the brothers of Joseph, and Aaron, and the brothers of David, and Absalom. I was the "other" brother—first and blessed but not chosen.

Soon after that my brother asked for his share of the inheritance. At first, the gall and impudence of his privileged entitlement burned within me. But the anger subsided when I learned that all he wanted was gold and silver and to travel to foreign lands. "Good riddance!" I said to myself. He could have the money. The land and the few servants who helped us work it was my share.

But the anger did not go away. It simply found another cause as I watched my father succumb to sadness. From the moment my brother walked away, Papa was a broken man. I could do nothing to restore any semblance of joy and wholeness to his life.

In time, Papa apathetically resigned the daily operation of our land to me. Mother and Sister managed even more of the household than before. A pall was cast over a once vibrant, passionate man. Papa may as well have walked down that road with my brother.

As for the prodigal, I heard stories from friends in Sepphoris of how he immediately squandered his inheritance on prostitutes, drunkenness, and dissolute living. The last they saw or heard of him was that he went with a trade caravan as a servant. I never bothered to tell Papa, thinking it would only break his heart further, if that were possible.

Then he came back, and so did the anger and even hatred not only toward him, but also at my Papa, whose shouts of joy cut through my heart like a sword.

Refusing to even go into the celebration, I sat at a distance and seethed. Papa eventually came pleading with me to come celebrate. Instead, I unleashed my anger at him.

"Listen! For all these years I worked like a slave for you, and I never disobeyed your command; yet you never gave me even a young goat so that I might celebrate with my friends. But when this son of yours who devoured your property with prostitutes came back, you killed the fatted calf for him!"

Then he said to me, "Son, you are always with me, and all that is mine is yours. But we must celebrate and rejoice, because this brother of yours was dead and now lives; he was lost and is now found."

His words fell into the pit of my hollow soul. I screamed silent words, "But don't you see the dead, lost son standing right in front of you?"

There was only one person I could go to in times like these. And I had one burning question for that person.

"Tell me about the angels, Mother." There was a long silence.

She took a deep breath. "I knew the day would come when you would ask."

I took a deep breath as well, preparing myself to hear something I didn't want to know. I was about to hear the story behind the secret exchange between my parents, "Remember the angels."

She spoke in the voice that meant *this is serious, pay close attention.* "The first thing you need to know, Jesus, is that what I am about to tell you only five people have known, three of whom are now dead—my cousin Elizabeth and your two grandmothers, may they rest in peace, your father, and me."

"I became pregnant with you before your father and I were actually married. We were engaged and had moments of intimacy but had not yet truly known one another." She paused and looked at me with vulnerability I had never seen in her.

"Please continue, Mother. I need to know."

"I really don't want to go into how I became pregnant, only Joseph knows that story. All you need to know is that at the time of our marriage, according to our Jewish law, your grandmothers did their duty by examining me, and to their horror, confirmed my secret suspicion."

"Which meant you were subject to punishment by death."

"Yes, and most likely Joseph as well. So, our mothers swore an oath to one another and to me that if Joseph would still marry me and be the father of my unborn child, the circumstances would be our secret forever."

"Joseph was shocked and angry, but most of all profoundly broken by my betrayal of our trust. As I told him things even our mothers didn't know, tears flowed down his face. He looked up in anguish then buried his face into his hands. He knew both of our lives were in jeopardy, but also said he felt as if his life had just been taken from him. He was also a man with great respect and honor for our law. I'll never forget what he said to me as we parted that day. 'Mary,' something in the way he said my name sounded so final, 'I don't know what we are to do, but whatever we do must be God's will and not ours.' As he turned and walked away I thought I would never see him again."

"That night I couldn't sleep. I cried and prayed. I even cursed God. Most of all I cursed myself. I finally fell asleep from physical and emotional exhaustion. That's when the angel appeared. Blinding light filled the room, and a voice came from the light. I'll never forget the words, 'Do not be afraid. I am here with you. You are safe.' Then the voice said something I had heard many mothers say about their children, but now rang with profound truth. 'The child forming in your womb will become a person of great wisdom, compassion, and love. Protect, nurture, and love this child with all your heart, soul, and body.' Then the voice and light were gone. I fell into deep, peaceful sleep knowing that somehow everything would be alright."

"Early the next morning Joseph was at my door. I wasn't the only one whose sleep had been interrupted. An angel of light had also visited him in his dreams. The angel told him also, 'Do not be afraid. I am here with you. You are safe.' And then the angel added, 'Do not be afraid to take Mary as your wife. The child in her womb is filled with God's Spirit. You will name him Jesus.'

"Suddenly our perspective shifted from fear for our own lives and reputations into doing what we needed to do in order for you to have life."

Mother stopped talking and looked at me as if waiting for a response. I was so overwhelmed with what I had just heard that I had no words.

Finally from somewhere deep inside beyond my thoughts and control, like someone else was speaking through me, words came from my mouth as if they had always been inside and were now erupting like lava from a volcano.

"Who is my father?"

"Your father is the man who has been with you from before birth, the man who witnessed your first breath, the man who gave you your name, the man who has sacrificed, sweated, and suffered for you, the man who provides for, cares for, and loves you, the man who calls you son is your father."

As I opened my mouth to speak, she held up her hand to stop me and added, "Jesus, the angels saved your life once, Joseph has done so many times, first out of duty and love for me, then from the moment he first held you it has been out of love for you."

The next morning before sunrise and without telling anyone, even my mother, I left home, and headed for Jerusalem.

Selah

~

In Jerusalem I never even entered the temple, much less offered sacrifice or prayers. Instead, I wandered the city streets for days and nights finding solace among the prostitutes and beggars.

For the first time in my life I lived among people whom I had always been taught were unclean sinners. They were the people I had walked past on the streets of Sepphoris and Jerusalem, the people who lived on city side streets and alleys I had never dared enter. And now I was one of them.

At first I was wary and suspicious of everyone, and they of me. I began to experience a culture and code entirely different from my own. They had been rejected and scorned by religious people, banned from the temple, and exploited by the rich and powerful. Even though my family was once poor, we always had shelter and enough food. And even though we lived under the oppression of the Romans, we had the safety of inclusion in the religious community.

The more time I spent with those in the margins, the more I began to identify with them. I heard their stories of desperation and dreams of hope. Many of the women who survived by selling their bodies told stories similar to the one I had so recently heard from my own mother. Had my grandmothers not protected Mother and Joseph, one of the men who begged and stole could have easily been him. I often wondered, if Joseph is not my father, could my father be within this culture of outcast sinners. Could these people be my family?

Most of all, during those days on the streets of Jerusalem I felt as if my life was hollow like an empty jar, void of meaning and purpose. Empty days became empty weeks until one day my purse was empty and I had to decide whether to give up or get out.

If there was one thing Joseph instilled in me it was the value and virtue of work. From an early age I learned from my father's word and example that, whatever the job, working hard and treating people fairly would benefit me in the long run. As I got older, he and I sometimes had different opinions as to what was "hard" and "fair," but the essential lesson stayed with me.

Now, outside the security of his household and without any money it was important to me to earn my own way. It was time to go to work, to have my own life. Unfortunately it was not always easy to do.

Every village and city has its own version of a temporary labor pool in which landowners and managers go to the local marketplace and hire men to work for them. This is especially true during harvesttime for various fruits and grains.

Even artisans like my father sometimes needed extra help with large jobs. When he did, he sent me to the market in Nazareth to hire workers.

So it was strange to find myself early one morning on the other side of this transaction, hungry and looking for work in the marketplace of another village.

Men milled about in gray predawn light, talking in low voices about who might need helpers that day. I knew it was the right place. In a short time a man approached with a confident stride and broke the muffled tones with a clear loud voice.

"I need four men to work in a vineyard today for the usual daily wage."

Before I realized what was happening the rest of the men straightened up and stepped forward. The man quickly pointed out four of them.

"Come with me."

Then they were gone. The hunger in my belly twisted tighter, fed only by disappointment.

"Will there be another?" I asked one of the remaining men.

"Sometimes, yes. Sometimes, no. All we can do is wait."

The sun melted away the morning coolness. We managed to find the shade and wait.

About nine o'clock the same man showed up again. This time everyone, not expecting the same man to need more workers, was caught off guard.

"I need four more men." Before anyone could volunteer he pointed at the four men nearest him and said. "Go into the vineyard, and I will pay you whatever is right."

Too soon the sun was high and hot when the man appeared in the marketplace again. This time I saw him coming and stood so I could respond quickly, but he walked right past me and without even asking pointed out four more men.

"The work is more than we anticipated. Go into the vineyard, and I will pay you whatever is right."

Word must have gotten around the village because just after noon more men began to show up in the marketplace and by afternoon as many men were waiting as had been early that morning.

Sure enough, around three o'clock, the vineyard manager came to the market place. I saw him coming and stood up only to be overrun by the other men who rushed toward him. He took six men, offering the same agreement to pay whatever was right, which we all understood to be a fourth of a day's wage.

When the man left with the six workers so did everyone else, except me. I found a shade which was now on the other side of the market, lay down and closed my eyes, hoping sleep would distract from my hunger.

"Why are you still here?" A familiar voice awakened me. It was the vineyard manager.

"Because no one has hired me."

"Have you been here all day?" he asked.

"Yes, but you never chose me. And now the day is gone."

Then to my great surprise, "There is still light, perhaps an hour of work remaining. You also go into the vineyard and I will pay you whatever is right."

An hour's wage would at least buy enough bread to get me through another day.

When I arrived at the vineyard the foreman pointed me to a section in the back that required me to walk past every one of the men who had been hired throughout the day. I could feel their stares and hear their suppressed laughter. I had hardly begun to get into a rhythm of work before the sun had set.

The manager shouted, "The day is done, men. Everyone line up here for your pay. Arrange yourselves beginning with those that came at five o'clock and then going to those who were first to work.

Then the landowner began paying us. I, being the only one to come at five o'clock, was first in line. The landowner handed me the usual daily wage.

"There must be some mistake, sir," I said. "Those who have worked all day are at the other end of the line."

"I've made no mistake," was all he said.

Then he proceeded down the line of men—three o'clock, noon, and nine o'clock—and everyone got a full day's wages while thinking the same thing, "Shouldn't those who worked more get paid more?"

Those at the end of the line who had worked all day were thinking the same and became visibly excited. We even heard one of them say, "Surely we will receive more, perhaps even double since we worked all day."

But their excitement was soon tempered and then dashed as the landowner handed them the usual daily wage, the same as everyone else.

They all began to grumble until one of them spoke up and pointed at me, "That man worked only one hour, and the rest of these only part of the day. You have made them equal to us who have borne the burden of the day and the scorching heat."

The landowner replied calmly yet firmly, "Friend, I am doing you no wrong; did you not agree with me for the usual daily wage? Take what belongs to you and go; I choose to give to this last the same as I give to you. Am I not allowed to do what I choose with what belongs to me? Or are you envious because I am generous?"

Selah

So began years of itinerate work as a field and vineyard laborer. One of the advantages, and sometimes curses, of repetitious, boring work is the time to think, ponder, and remember. Even though I had left my family, the memory of them and our life together was my constant companion.

I eventually became a manager for the vineyard owner who hired me that day and paid me a day's wage for an hour's work. After working for him from the labor pool for a while, he hired me as a permanent worker. I soon discovered he was a very wealthy landowner and had many vineyards and wheat fields. It wasn't long before he put me in charge of a one of his vineyards. This meant I had to hire my own workers from the labor pool, and to account to the owner for the harvest. I was no longer paid an hourly wage but a percentage of the harvest.

Using his example of generosity from that first day I was generous to those who worked for me. Because of this I was never short of good workers. However, my own generosity eventually became my near downfall.

In time, because so many people wanted to work for me, the landowner made me supervisor over several vineyards, as well as wheat fields, each of which had its own manager. It was my job to make sure each individual vineyard or field manager produced as much as possible for the owner. I also insisted that this not be done at the expense of their workers, that they were treated fairly and paid generously. In turn, I was generous with the managers in allowing them flexibility in their payments to the owner. This is where it all began to turn.

One of the managers who worked under me had also been part of the labor pool on that first day. He was one of those who had worked all day and had complained about being treated unfairly. Even still he also became a regular worker for the landowner, and eventually manager of his own vineyard.

We became competitors. Both of us were top producers for the landowner, but by very different methods. In short, his profits came at the expense of his workers, who were overworked, underpaid, and disposable. Where I tried to develop permanent workers, he continually used the labor pool.

When I became his supervisor, there was disagreement between us. However, his bottom line was always a profit, which pleased the landowner, and so the landowner also made him supervisor in charge of several other managers. This meant he was no longer under my supervision.

One day this man went to the landowner and accused me of squandering his property. The landowner summoned me and said, "What is this I hear about you? Give me an account of your management."

My accounting showed that several of my managers were overdue in paying their expected quotas. I explained to the landowner that I was only following his example of generosity in giving the managers some flexibility with their payments so they could provide for themselves, their workers, and their families.

The landowner said words I had heard before but never directed at me. "You seem to have forgotten something about me. Am I not allowed to do what I choose with what belongs to me? Take what little belongs to you and go because you cannot be my manager any longer." As quick as that, I was only a few days' provision away from being back in the labor pool myself.

Then I said to myself, "What will I do, now that the landowner is taking the position away from me?" Surprisingly, I also thought, "What would Father do?"

I knew one thing for certain, even if I was dismissed, I could help the people who had worked under me settle with the landowner. Hopefully, in return, they would welcome me into their homes and perhaps even hire me as one of their workers.

So, summoning them one by one, I asked the first, "How much do you owe my master?"

He answered, "A hundred jugs of olive oil."

"Take your bill, sit down quickly, and make it fifty."

Then I asked another, "And how much do you owe?"

He replied, "A hundred containers of wheat."

"Take your bill and make it eighty."

So it was with every manager, each willing to pay as much as he could.

When we delivered the goods to the landowner he was surprised, first to even see me again, and second at receiving what he had already counted as lost.

"I commend you," he said. "You are indeed a shrewd manager. Your position is again secure."

Not only did I regain my position, in the process of doing so, people who once were managers who worked for me were now true friends for life.

Selah

L ife has taught me that just when I think I am settled and secure something or someone comes along to disturb and unsettle my security. I was finally living my own life as a property manager, enjoying friends, and rarely thinking of my former life at home. I was building my own home. Then one day I overheard a stranger talking about a bizarre man who lived in the Jordan wilderness south of Jericho, dressed in animal skins, ate wild honey and insects to survive, and proclaimed the teachings of the prophet Isaiah. Evidently many people were becoming his disciples and being baptized in the Jordan River.

This was nothing new. There were always people claiming to be this or that prophet to stir up people against the Romans. Then someone said the man's name was John!

My cousin John had disappeared a few years before my brother James had taken his inheritance and left. We even thought at one time that perhaps James had gone to find John. This was put to rest when we heard that John had joined a commune of ascetic, religious zealots called the Essenes, which was not James' style at all. The occasional rumor would surface about John and his whereabouts, but no one really knew.

Something deep inside told me this wilderness preacher at the Jordan River was my cousin. For no more reason than this, I turned over my business affairs to a trusted friend to manage. I had to find out if this wilderness preacher was my cousin John.

I gathered provisions and enough money for a few weeks and headed for the Jordan River by way of Jericho.

Selah

~

. . . I never saw the Stranger again even though the inn-keeper said that when I was asleep he had showed up to pay for my expenses. However, I did see him every time I closed my eyes, his face shining with pure light, his eyes looking into my soul.

More importantly, I heard his comforting words. "Don't be afraid. You are safe." And then the haunting ones, "You were lost but now found, dead but now alive."

As haunting as the words were, they were also true. I had been lost and would have died on that road to Jericho, but the stranger found me and gave me new life. Now I also realized that even before meeting those bandits I was lost in fear and anger toward my brother and Papa. I was dead in spirit, unworthy and unable to give or receive kindness or love from anyone.

As my broken body slowly healed I also noticed a change in spirit. When the innkeeper brought me a meal or changed a bandage, I felt as if the Stranger were in the room. In a flashing moment the innkeeper's eyes shone brief glimpses of the Stranger's eyes. Occasionally his voice resonated with the same all-encompassing comfort as the Stranger's.

Once while I slept in the middle of the afternoon the Stranger came to me in a dream so real I still wonder to this day if he wasn't actually there. The now familiar soothing light filled his face, extending to illuminate everything, including me. Surprisingly my faced burned hot but not with the peace I had come to know from the Stranger. I was hot with anger and realized the Stranger's face had become the faces of my brother and Papa who somehow seemed separate yet the same person. My anger was more intense than ever before. My face and head throbbed to release it but it wouldn't come out. Then came the Stranger's voice, "Breathe and swallow."

"Don't be afraid. You are safe. You always have been." I took a deep breath and swallowed. A suffocating mask lifted from my face. The roaring fire in my head moved down my throat, through my body, and into my belly—still burning hot. It churned in my gut as it transformed from anger into fear and pain. Then deep within my bowels my fear and pain became the fear and pain of my Papa and brother. The anger was gone. All I wanted was to be with them, to reach out and touch them and say, "I was lost but now I'm found, dead but now I'm alive."

First I had to find my cousin John.

Selah

Arriving at the Jordan River, I saw the person who people that passed through the inn had described, a man with long disheveled hair and beard, covered in animal skins. He did not look like my cousin. But when he spoke I knew it was John.

There were several hundred people from all walks of life gathered around him as he preached from atop a large stone beside a wide place in the Jordan River where a pool was formed. He talked about change, about turning away from greed and extortion and oppression, and instead living generously, equitably, and compassionately.

He told of sharing with the poor, treating one another fairly, and liberating captive people. The stories were interspersed with quotes from scripture, mostly the prophet Isaiah. His message stirred within me, as had the words of the Stranger and the innkeeper. An aura began to form around him that soon became that familiar light inviting me to enter. As the light grew larger and brighter, all awareness of the other people faded away as did John's words. Soon there was only light surrounding us. We were not only in the light we were the light. Then the light spoke.

"Don't be afraid. You are safe. You are loved. You are light. You are love. You always have been." Then the light was gone. John's voice returned.

"Jesus! I've been waiting for you! What took you so long?"

"What?" How did he know I was coming to see him? Why was I now soaking wet, standing in the Jordan River up to my waist? Why were all the people shouting my name and cheering?

"What's going on, John?"

"Don't say anything now." His voice had changed from the bombastic, assured tone of his preaching to hushed reverence. "We need to get you away from this crowd and talk about what just happened."

Selah

John's voice came from the flames of the fire between us. "So tell me your story, from as far back as you can remember."

As I finished talking the roaring fire that had at first hidden John's face was now a gentle rolling flame above a bed of hot coals that lit his face with a red glow.

After a long silence, I said, "That's my story, John. There are many other stories I could tell, but these are the ones that tell you who I think I am."

"We are our stories, Jesus, the ones we tell as well as the ones that stay hidden."

"What about you, John? What is your story?"

John then shared a story that was all too familiar of how after leaving Nazareth years before he had wandered aimlessly, working odd jobs here and there, until he was taken in by an Essene community near the Dead Sea. For the next several years he lived a life of separation, simplicity, and study in the desert.

"These people invited me into their community and treated me with kindness and respect," he said. "They also taught me a new understanding of the scriptures, especially the prophet Isaiah."

"What was so different? I asked.

"It was how they brought Isaiah's words into our present situation, how our living under the thumb of Rome and their temple puppets is no different than that of our ancestors in Babylon."

"I hear that kind of talk and that same comparison from zealots everywhere these days, John," I replied.

"Agreed," John said. "But the difference comes in how to combat the oppression. They say Isaiah's 'Day of the Lord' is already here. They taught me that the way to freedom and liberation is not through open conflict and might, but rather through sharing our possessions with those who have nothing, treating people with kindness, and compassion and giving people their dignity."

"This all sounds good, John," I said, "but do you really expect to overcome the brutality and greed of Rome and the temple with kindness and compassion?"

"Not Rome or the temple, Jesus. I'm talking about our own people, you and me." John continued about how living under oppression had hardened our hearts and drained our souls of the humility, justice, and kindness that the prophets taught. He explained how he left the Essenes and lived alone in the desert for two years.

"One cold, clear desert night much like tonight when the stars are within reach the prophet Isaiah spoke to me. 'John, you are a voice in the wilderness of humanity. Go and proclaim that the time when the poor are given hope, the naked clothed, the hungry fed, and the captive freed is near. One is coming to show us the way. Proclaim this good news to a people hungry to hear it.'"

As John spoke he looked into my soul. The reflection of fire danced in the darkness of his eyes until he again became the flame. This time the voice was not John's, but the Stranger's, "Jesus, you are the one to show us the way."

The flame returned to the reflection in John's eyes as his voice returned, "Jesus, my cousin, I believe you are the one we are waiting for, you are the Messiah."

He paused to let his words penetrate, and then he continued, "When I saw you in the crowd today your face shone with a bright light that quickly engulfed me as you walked toward me and into the river. As I poured water over your head, I heard a voice say, "Follow him. He will show you the way."

"But, John, I'm just a man like you. How could. . ."

He held up his hand to silence me. "I know it sounds crazy. My first thought was, 'Surely it can't be my cousin, Jesus!' Yet, I also know with all my being it is true."

"But how do I know it's true?" I insisted.

"Go into the wilderness alone and listen to your life. Listen to the story you told me tonight. By listening you will discover angels of your own to remember."

"I suspect I've already encountered a few around this fire tonight, John. Perhaps those two thieves on the road to Jericho were angels in disguise."

"Yes!" A big smile crossed John's face. "Now you're on the right path. Even in suffering and darkness you will discover the Presence and Light of God within yourself. Then, above all else, don't be afraid to be who you are. You will find the way in which you are to lead," he said with conviction.

Through a mischievous smile I remembered from our childhood he said, "Who knows? One day perhaps I will hear stories of Isaiah's vision alive among our people."

The following morning I packed a few provisions and walked into a wilderness of rocks, sun, and endless sky, but also into the wilderness of memory and imagination where the past becomes the future.

The sun shone bright and hot not unlike that morning I had walked the road from Jerusalem to Jericho. I looked into its blaze and heard a familiar voice from within, "Don't be afraid. I am here with you. You are safe. You are not who you think you are. You are light, the light of the world."

Selah

The Dénouement

For many years the primal story of my life was the death of my father when I was sixteen years old. From the moment "Daddy" died my life, both before and after, was changed. However, more recently a different story has emerged as a primal story in my life, a story that in many ways sheds light on why telling the story and stories of Jesus is central in my own calling and vocation.

As an eight-year-old boy I responded to an altar call at a revival meeting in the Southern Baptist congregation of my youth and announced I was called to be a preacher. My parents, even though deeply religious and proud of me, didn't know what to do. Our pastor gave them what seemed at the time rather odd advice, "Just as you do with all of your children, nurture him in a Christian home and keep him in your prayers. But, never specifically mention this incident to him again. If the call is true, someday he will come to you." So they never mentioned it again. Nearly thirty years later when I called my mother to tell her I was thinking about entering seminary, she told me the story above.

A month before I graduated from seminary my mother died. She didn't have a formal will but had instead taken a spiral notebook and created a page for each of her children on which she listed the things of hers she wanted us to have, none of which had much monetary value, but all sentimental treasures. One of the things on my list was an old steamer trunk filled with various smaller boxes containing letters, photos, old newspaper clippings, small keepsakes, and even yellowing school report cards. Toward the bottom of the box I found a tattered construction paper booklet held together by cotton string. On the front cover in large, red crayon and childlike lettering was, "'All About Me' by Andy W." Inside on the first page, in obviously novice cursive handwriting, I had written, "I am eight years old." Three pages later, following a traced hand complete with Timex watch and ring were these chilling words, "This is what I want to be when I grow up. I would like to be a preacher because I want to tell people about Jesus . . ."

After pastoring, preaching, and teaching for over twenty years, one day I picked up that tattered construction paper booklet and the words "tell people about Jesus" spoke to me anew. The Jesus I have discovered and want to tell people about is not the Jesus of my childhood who had to die to save me and the world from eternal damnation, but rather a flesh-and-blood person who lived a Divinely infused life that leads us to discover, experience, and live the Divine in our lives. And he does this by being fully human.

Hearing the stories of Jesus as his own personal stories makes Jesus more real, accessible, and present than ever before in my life, inviting and allowing me to reinterpret and reimagine some of the evangelical language of my youth, like "personal relationship with Jesus," or accepting Jesus as my "friend." These are no longer shallow, sentimental platitudes, but rather windows into the depth and profundity of shared humanity and incarnate divinity.

As author Fr. Richard Rohr says, "Jesus came precisely to put it all together for us and in us. He was saying, in effect, 'to be human is good! The material and the physical can be trusted and enjoyed. This world is the hiding place of God and the revelation of God!"[1]

My sincere and simple hope is that by allowing a more human Jesus to "come to Light" in his stories you begin to see the Light of Life hidden in your own stories.

---

1. Rohr, *Everything Belongs: The Gift of Contemplative Prayer* (New York: Crossroad, 2003), 117–19.

Postlude

Dried blood and sweat fill my eyes. Each breath entering my throbbing chest is more and more shallow. Every attempt to move my arms or legs produces pure anguish. How long will it take for life to slowly drain from my body? Am I to die beaten, bloodied, naked, and alone in the scorching sun?

My eyes close. The ringing in my head subsides to the hum of insect wings in my ears as they crawl about my face, but I can do nothing. The sun beats down upon me, yet cold wells up within. I begin to shiver.

With a gasping breath my body stills, the pain gone. "So, this is death?" Darkness gently caresses me. Then silence.

In the dark distance a light moves toward me. Or am I moving toward the light? I have no way of knowing for all points of reference are gone. The light grows larger and brighter and at some point I see a figure within the light, inviting me into the light. There are no words yet I can hear a voice within, "Don't be afraid. I am here with you. You are safe." The voice fills me with peace and wholeness.

Shovels and picks are digging and voices complaining, "How much deeper must we dig?"

"Until you hit rock. We don't want it to fall down," Papa says to James and me.

Then comes another voice, sinister and sarcastic, "Don't want it to fall. They might get hurt!" followed by laughter.

"Get those two timbers," Papa says. "Tie the small one across the large one at right angle and secure it with a nail." Hammers pound away.

The shovels and picks stop digging. "We're at the bottom."

"Are you sure?" someone asks.

"No, don't stop now," Papa says. "It's here I know it is. Keep digging."

"Father, forgive them, they know not what they do."

A man's voice rips the air, "Save yourself and save us!" Another, gentler voice responds, "Leave him alone. He's done nothing to you."

I turn toward the compassion. The man's face is hidden in silhouette, the bright sun behind him. The course voice continues ranting. Both voices seem familiar.

"The cloak is mine," one says.

"I'll take the sandals," says another.

Then comes a third more commanding voice from below, "No! We wager."

The silhouetted face speaks again in a voice from another time and place, another silhouette on a dusty road. "Forgive us."

"Speak for yourself, fool," barks the angry voice. "Who is he to forgive? He's a common thief just like us."

"Don't be afraid." The voice from the light fills the air yet comes from my swollen tongue. The words I speak are so familiar. "You are not alone. You are safe. I am with you. You are not who you think you are. You are light, the light of the world."

"This day you will be with me in Paradise."

Voices and sounds blend into a cacophony penetrating the recesses of my soul. I am in the tiny house of my youth. Mother is alone, busily preparing our evening meal. She reaches into her cloak for a small pouch of salt and as she does a single coin falls unnoticed from her cloak. The coin remains suspended in air as she puts a pinch of salt in the dough she kneads. Then the coin continues to the floor with the jingling sound of many coins being shaken in a purse. It rolls across the floor into a dark corner crevice just big enough to obscure it from sight, waiting to be found.

"Woman, behold your son."

I cry out. The words are mine from deep within, yet I hear them as if someone else speaks them from another time and place. They fill the air with fear and pain, my fear and pain.

"My God, my God, why have you forsaken me?"

I feel coolness on my forehead. Someone washes my face. At first the wetness sooths my parched lips, then the smell and taste of bitter wine snatches me back into scorching heat and cavernous pain.

"I thirst."

The light returns. It is a flame. John's face appears, "Don't be afraid to be who you are!"

The flame becomes pure light, pure kindness, compassion, and love. I enter the light and in doing so, become the light. It grows blindingly bright. Its heat penetrates my soul. A voice, my voice says, "Don't be afraid. I am you. You are I. We are One."

"It is finished."

I am not afraid. I know I am safe for I am the Presence.

"Into your hands I commit my spirit."

Selah

Appendix

The Good Samaritan, Luke 10:25–37

25 Just then a lawyer stood up to test Jesus. "Teacher," he said, "what must I do to inherit eternal life?" 26 He said to him, "What is written in the law? What do you read there?" 27 He answered, "You shall love the Lord your God with all your heart, and with all your soul, and with all your strength, and with all your mind; and your neighbor as yourself." 28 And he said to him, "You have given the right answer; do this, and you will live."

29 But wanting to justify himself, he asked Jesus, "And who is my neighbor?" 30 Jesus replied, "A man was going down from Jerusalem to Jericho, and fell into the hands of robbers, who stripped him, beat him, and went away, leaving him half dead. 31 Now by chance a priest was going down that road; and when he saw him, he passed by on the other side. 32 So likewise a Levite, when he came to the place and saw him, passed by on the other side. 33 But a Samaritan while traveling came near him; and when he saw him, he was moved with pity. 34 He went to him and bandaged his wounds, having poured oil and wine on them. Then he put him on his own animal, brought him to an

inn, and took care of him. 35 The next day he took out two denarii, gave them to the innkeeper, and said, 'Take care of him; and when I come back, I will repay you whatever more you spend.' 36 Which of these three, do you think, was a neighbor to the man who fell into the hands of the robbers?" 37 He said, "The one who showed him mercy." Jesus said to him, "Go and do likewise."

The Lost Coin, Luke 15:8–10

8 "Or what woman having ten silver coins, if she loses one of them, does not light a lamp, sweep the house, and search carefully until she finds it? 9 When she has found it, she calls together her friends and neighbors, saying, 'Rejoice with me, for I have found the coin that I had lost.' 10 Just so, I tell you, there is joy in the presence of the angels of God over one sinner who repents."

The Leaven, Luke 13:20–21 (also Matthew 13:33)

20 And again he said, "To what should I compare the kingdom of God? 21 It is like yeast that a woman took and mixed in with three measures of flour until all of it was leavened."

Jesus Twelve Years Old at the Temple, Luke 2:41–52

41 Now every year his parents went to Jerusalem for the festival of the Passover. 42 And when he was twelve years old, they went up as usual for the festival. 43 When the festival was ended and they started to return, the boy Jesus stayed behind in Jerusalem, but his parents did not know it. 44

Assuming that he was in the group of travelers, they went a day's journey. Then they started to look for him among their relatives and friends. 45 When they did not find him, they returned to Jerusalem to search for him. 46 After three days they found him in the temple, sitting among the teachers, listening to them and asking them questions. 47 And all who heard him were amazed at his understanding and his answers. 48 When his parents saw him they were astonished; and his mother said to him, "Child, why have you treated us like this? Look, your father and I have been searching for you in great anxiety." 49 He said to them, "Why were you searching for me? Did you not know that I must be in my Father's house?" 50 But they did not understand what he said to them. 51 Then he went down with them and came to Nazareth, and was obedient to them. His mother treasured all these things in her heart.

52 And Jesus increased in wisdom and in years, and in divine and human favor.

The Two Builders, Luke 6:47–49 (also Matthew 7:24–27)

47 I will show you what someone is like who comes to me, hears my words, and acts on them. 48 That one is like a man building a house, who dug deeply and laid the foundation on rock; when a flood arose, the river burst against that house but could not shake it, because it had been well built. 49 But the one who hears and does not act is like a man who built a house on the ground without a foundation. When the river burst against it, immediately it fell, and great was the ruin of that house.

The Net, Matthew 13:47–50

47 Again, the kingdom of heaven is like a net that was thrown into the sea and caught fish of every kind; 48 when it was full, they drew it ashore, sat down, and put the good into baskets but threw out the bad. 49 So it will be at the end of the age. The angels will come out and separate the evil from the righteous 50 and throw them into the furnace of fire, where there will be weeping and gnashing of teeth.

The Mustard Seed, Luke 13:18–19 (also Matthew 13:31–32; Mark 4:30–32)

18 He said therefore, "What is the kingdom of God like? And to what should I compare it? 19 It is like a mustard seed that someone took and sowed in the garden; it grew and became a tree, and the birds of the air made nests in its branches."

The Hidden Treasure, Matthew 13:44

44 The kingdom of heaven is like treasure hidden in a field, which someone found and hid; then in his joy he goes and sells all that he has and buys that field.

Joseph's Dreams and Escape to and from Egypt, Matthew 2:13–15, 19–23

13 Now after they had left, an angel of the Lord appeared to Joseph in a dream and said, "Get up, take the child and his mother, and flee to Egypt, and remain there until I tell you; for Herod is about to search for the child, to destroy him." 14 Then Joseph got up, took the child and his mother by

night, and went to Egypt, 15 and remained there until the death of Herod. This was to fulfill what had been spoken by the Lord through the prophet, "Out of Egypt I have called my son."

19 When Herod died, an angel of the Lord suddenly appeared in a dream to Joseph in Egypt and said, 20 "Get up, take the child and his mother, and go to the land of Israel, for those who were seeking the child's life are dead." 21 Then Joseph got up, took the child and his mother, and went to the land of Israel. 22 But when he heard that Archelaus was ruling over Judea in place of his father Herod, he was afraid to go there. And after being warned in a dream, he went away to the district of Galilee. 23 There he made his home in a town called Nazareth, so that what had been spoken through the prophets might be fulfilled, "He will be called a Nazorean."

The Lost Sheep, Luke 15:3–7 (also Matthew 18:12–14)

3 So he told them this parable: 4 "Which one of you, having a hundred sheep and losing one of them, does not leave the ninety-nine in the wilderness and go after the one that is lost until he finds it? 5 When he has found it, he lays it on his shoulders and rejoices. 6 And when he comes home, he calls together his friends and neighbors, saying to them, 'Rejoice with me, for I have found my sheep that was lost.' 7 Just so, I tell you, there will be more joy in heaven over one sinner who repents than over ninety-nine righteous persons who need no repentance."

The Prodigal Son, Luke 15:11–32

11 Then Jesus said, "There was a man who had two sons. 12 The younger of them said to his father, 'Father, give me the share of the property that will belong to me.' So he divided his property between them. 13 A few days later the younger son gathered all he had and traveled to a distant country, and there he squandered his property in dissolute living. 14 When he had spent everything, a severe famine took place throughout that country, and he began to be in need. 15 So he went and hired himself out to one of the citizens of that country, who sent him to his fields to feed the pigs. 16 He would gladly have filled himself with the pods that the pigs were eating; and no one gave him anything. 17 But when he came to himself he said, 'How many of my father's hired hands have bread enough and to spare, but here I am dying of hunger! 18 I will get up and go to my father, and I will say to him, "Father, I have sinned against heaven and before you; 19 I am no longer worthy to be called your son; treat me like one of your hired hands."' 20 So he set off and went to his father. But while he was still far off, his father saw him and was filled with compassion; he ran and put his arms around him and kissed him. 21 Then the son said to him, 'Father, I have sinned against heaven and before you; I am no longer worthy to be called your son.' 22 But the father said to his slaves, 'Quickly, bring out a robe—the best one—and put it on him; put a ring on his finger and sandals on his feet. 23 And get the fatted calf and kill it, and let us eat and celebrate; 24 for this son of mine was dead and is alive again; he was lost and is found!' And they began to celebrate.

25 "Now his elder son was in the field; and when he came and approached the house, he heard music and dancing. 26 He called one of the slaves and asked what was going

on. 27 He replied, 'Your brother has come, and your father has killed the fatted calf, because he has got him back safe and sound.' 28 Then he became angry and refused to go in. His father came out and began to plead with him. 29 But he answered his father, 'Listen! For all these years I have been working like a slave for you, and I have never disobeyed your command; yet you have never given me even a young goat so that I might celebrate with my friends. 30 But when this son of yours came back, who has devoured your property with prostitutes, you killed the fatted calf for him!' 31 Then the father said to him, 'Son, you are always with me, and all that is mine is yours. 32 But we had to celebrate and rejoice, because this brother of yours was dead and has come to life; he was lost and has been found.'"

Jesus' Conception, Luke 1:26–37

26 In the sixth month the angel Gabriel was sent by God to a town in Galilee called Nazareth, 27 to a virgin engaged to a man whose name was Joseph, of the house of David. The virgin's name was Mary. 28 And he came to her and said, "Greetings, favored one! The Lord is with you." 29 But she was much perplexed by his words and pondered what sort of greeting this might be. 30 The angel said to her, "Do not be afraid, Mary, for you have found favor with God. 31 And now, you will conceive in your womb and bear a son, and you will name him Jesus. 32 He will be great, and will be called the Son of the Most High, and the Lord God will give to him the throne of his ancestor David. 33 He will reign over the house of Jacob forever, and of his kingdom there will be no end." 34 Mary said to the angel, "How can this be, since I am a virgin?" 35 The angel said to her, "The Holy Spirit will come upon you, and the power of the Most High will overshadow you; therefore the child to be born will be

holy; he will be called Son of God. 36 And now, your relative Elizabeth in her old age has also conceived a son; and this is the sixth month for her who was said to be barren. 37 For nothing will be impossible with God." 38 Then Mary said, "Here am I, the servant of the Lord; let it be with me according to your word." Then the angel departed from her.

Jesus' Conception, Matthew 1:18–25

18 Now the birth of Jesus the Messiah took place in this way. When his mother Mary had been engaged to Joseph, but before they lived together, she was found to be with child from the Holy Spirit. 19 Her husband Joseph, being a righteous man and unwilling to expose her to public disgrace, planned to dismiss her quietly. 20 But just when he had resolved to do this, an angel of the Lord appeared to him in a dream and said, "Joseph, son of David, do not be afraid to take Mary as your wife, for the child conceived in her is from the Holy Spirit. 21 She will bear a son, and you are to name him Jesus, for he will save his people from their sins." 22 All this took place to fulfill what had been spoken by the Lord through the prophet:

23 "Look, the virgin shall conceive and bear a son,
and they shall name him Emmanuel,"
which means, "God is with us."

24 When Joseph awoke from sleep, he did as the angel of the Lord commanded him; he took her as his wife, 25 but had no marital relations with her until she had borne a son; and he named him Jesus.

The Laborers in the Vineyard,
Matthew 20:1–16

"For the kingdom of heaven is like a landowner who went out early in the morning to hire laborers for his vineyard. 2 After agreeing with the laborers for the usual daily wage, he sent them into his vineyard. 3 When he went out about nine o'clock, he saw others standing idle in the marketplace; 4 and he said to them, 'You also go into the vineyard, and I will pay you whatever is right.' So they went. 5 When he went out again about noon and about three o'clock, he did the same. 6 And about five o'clock he went out and found others standing around; and he said to them, 'Why are you standing here idle all day?' 7 They said to him, 'Because no one has hired us.' He said to them, 'You also go into the vineyard.' 8 When evening came, the owner of the vineyard said to his manager, 'Call the laborers and give them their pay, beginning with the last and then going to the first.' 9 When those hired about five o'clock came, each of them received the usual daily wage. 10 Now when the first came, they thought they would receive more; but each of them also received the usual daily wage. 11 And when they received it, they grumbled against the landowner, 12 saying, 'These last worked only one hour, and you have made them equal to us who have borne the burden of the day and the scorching heat.' 13 But he replied to one of them, 'Friend, I am doing you no wrong; did you not agree with me for the usual daily wage? 14 Take what belongs to you and go; I choose to give to this last the same as I give to you. 15 Am I not allowed to do what I choose with what belongs to me? Or are you envious because I am generous?' 16 So the last will be first, and the first will be last."

Appendix

The Dishonest Steward, Luke 16:1–12

Then Jesus said to the disciples, "There was a rich man who had a manager, and charges were brought to him that this man was squandering his property. 2 So he summoned him and said to him, 'What is this that I hear about you? Give me an accounting of your management, because you cannot be my manager any longer.' 3 Then the manager said to himself, 'What will I do, now that my master is taking the position away from me? I am not strong enough to dig, and I am ashamed to beg. 4 I have decided what to do so that, when I am dismissed as manager, people may welcome me into their homes.' 5 So, summoning his master's debtors one by one, he asked the first, 'How much do you owe my master?' 6 He answered, 'A hundred jugs of olive oil.' He said to him, 'Take your bill, sit down quickly, and make it fifty.' 7 Then he asked another, 'And how much do you owe?' He replied, 'A hundred containers of wheat.' He said to him, 'Take your bill and make it eighty.' 8 And his master commended the dishonest manager because he had acted shrewdly; for the children of this age are more shrewd in dealing with their own generation than are the children of light. 9 And I tell you, make friends for yourselves by means of dishonest wealth so that when it is gone, they may welcome you into the eternal homes.

10 "Whoever is faithful in a very little is faithful also in much; and whoever is dishonest in a very little is dishonest also in much. 11 If then you have not been faithful with the dishonest wealth, who will entrust to you the true riches? 12 And if you have not been faithful with what belongs to another, who will give you what is your own? 13 No slave can serve two masters; for a slave will either hate the one and love the other, or be devoted to the one and despise the other. You cannot serve God and wealth."

*John the Baptist and Jesus' Baptism, Luke 3:1–
22; 4:1 (also Matthew 3:1—4:1; Mark 1:1-2;
John 1:19-34)*

In the fifteenth year of the reign of Emperor Tiberius, when
Pontius Pilate was governor of Judea, and Herod was ruler
of Galilee, and his brother Philip ruler of the region of Itu-
raea and Trachonitis, and Lysanias ruler of Abilene, 2 during the high priesthood of Annas and Caiaphas, the word
of God came to John son of Zechariah in the wilderness. 3
He went into all the region around the Jordan, proclaiming
a baptism of repentance for the forgiveness of sins, 4 as it is
written in the book of the words of the prophet Isaiah,

> The voice of one crying out in the wilderness:
> "Prepare the way of the Lord,
>   make his paths straight.
> 5 Every valley shall be filled,
>   and every mountain and hill shall be made low,
> and the crooked shall be made straight,
>   and the rough ways made smooth;
> 6 and all flesh shall see the salvation of God."

7 John said to the crowds that came out to be baptized
by him, "You brood of vipers! Who warned you to flee from
the wrath to come? 8 Bear fruits worthy of repentance. Do
not begin to say to yourselves, 'We have Abraham as our
ancestor'; for I tell you, God is able from these stones to
raise up children to Abraham. 9 Even now the ax is lying at
the root of the trees; every tree therefore that does not bear
good fruit is cut down and thrown into the fire."

10 And the crowds asked him, "What then should we
do?" 11 In reply he said to them, "Whoever has two coats
must share with anyone who has none; and whoever has
food must do likewise." 12 Even tax collectors came to be
baptized, and they asked him, "Teacher, what should we

do?" 13 He said to them, "Collect no more than the amount prescribed for you." 14 Soldiers also asked him, "And we, what should we do?" He said to them, "Do not extort money from anyone by threats or false accusation, and be satisfied with your wages."

15 As the people were filled with expectation, and all were questioning in their hearts concerning John, whether he might be the Messiah, 16 John answered all of them by saying, "I baptize you with water; but one who is more powerful than I is coming; I am not worthy to untie the thong of his sandals. He will baptize you with the Holy Spirit and fire. 17 His winnowing fork is in his hand, to clear his threshing floor and to gather the wheat into his granary; but the chaff he will burn with unquenchable fire."

18 So, with many other exhortations, he proclaimed the good news to the people. 19 But Herod the ruler, who had been rebuked by him because of Herodias, his brother's wife, and because of all the evil things that Herod had done, 20 added to them all by shutting up John in prison.

21 Now when all the people were baptized, and when Jesus also had been baptized and was praying, the heaven was opened, 22 and the Holy Spirit descended upon him in bodily form like a dove. And a voice came from heaven, "You are my Son, the Beloved; with you I am well pleased."

4:1 Jesus, full of the Holy Spirit, returned from the Jordan and was led by the Spirit in the wilderness,

The Crucifixion and Death of Jesus, Luke 23:26–49 (also Matthew 27:32–56; Mark 15:21–41; and John 19:16–37)

26 As they led him away, they seized a man, Simon of Cyrene, who was coming from the country, and they laid the cross on him, and made him carry it behind Jesus. 27 A

great number of the people followed him, and among them were women who were beating their breasts and wailing for him. 28 But Jesus turned to them and said, "Daughters of Jerusalem, do not weep for me, but weep for yourselves and for your children. 29 For the days are surely coming when they will say, 'Blessed are the barren, and the wombs that never bore, and the breasts that never nursed.' 30 Then they will begin to say to the mountains, 'Fall on us'; and to the hills, 'Cover us.' 31 For if they do this when the wood is green, what will happen when it is dry?"

32 Two others also, who were criminals, were led away to be put to death with him. 33 When they came to the place that is called The Skull, they crucified Jesus there with the criminals, one on his right and one on his left. 34 Then Jesus said, "Father, forgive them; for they do not know what they are doing." And they cast lots to divide his clothing. 35 And the people stood by, watching; but the leaders scoffed at him, saying, "He saved others; let him save himself if he is the Messiah of God, his chosen one!" 36 The soldiers also mocked him, coming up and offering him sour wine, 37 and saying, "If you are the King of the Jews, save yourself!" 38 There was also an inscription over him, "This is the King of the Jews."

39 One of the criminals who were hanged there kept deriding him and saying, "Are you not the Messiah? Save yourself and us!" 40 But the other rebuked him, saying, "Do you not fear God, since you are under the same sentence of condemnation? 41 And we indeed have been condemned justly, for we are getting what we deserve for our deeds, but this man has done nothing wrong." 42 Then he said, "Jesus, remember me when you come into your kingdom." 43 He replied, "Truly I tell you, today you will be with me in Paradise."

44 It was now about noon, and darkness came over the whole land until three in the afternoon, 45 while the sun's light failed; and the curtain of the temple was torn in two. 46 Then Jesus, crying with a loud voice, said, "Father, into your hands I commend my spirit." Having said this, he breathed his last. 47 When the centurion saw what had taken place, he praised God and said, "Certainly this man was innocent." 48 And when all the crowds who had gathered there for this spectacle saw what had taken place, they returned home, beating their breasts. 49 But all his acquaintances, including the women who had followed him from Galilee, stood at a distance, watching these things.

The Seven Last Words of Christ

Father, forgive them, for they do not know what they are doing. Luke 23:34

Today you will be with me in paradise. Luke 23:43

Woman, here is your son. John 19:26

My God, my God, why have you forsaken me? Matthew 27:46

I am thirsty. John 19:28

It is finished. John 19:30

Father, into your hands I commend my spirit. Luke 23:46